THE TECHNICS OF BEL CANTO

THE TECHNICS OF BEL CANTO

BY

GIOVANNI BATTISTA LAMPERTI

ISBN: 978-93-5128-785-8(HB)

First Published in 1905
Indian Reprint in 2017

Published by

Kalpaz Publications
C-30, Satyawati Nagar,
Delhi – 110052
E-mail: kalpaz@hotmail.com
Website: kalpazpublications.com
Ph.: +91-9212142040

Cataloging in Publication Data—DK
Courtesy: D.K. Agencies (P) Ltd. <docinfo@dkagencies.com>

Lamperti, Giovanni Battista, 1839-1910, **author.**
The technics of bel canto / by Giovanni Battista Lamperti.
pages cm
"First published in 1905"—Title page verso.
ISBN 9789351287858

1. Singing—Methods. 2. Singing—Instruction and study—Italy. 3. Bel canto. I. Title.

MT820.L36 2017 DDC 783 23

PREFACE

It appears superfluous and aimless to add a new singing-method to those already before the public. However, during many years devoted to lesson-giving, I have observed far too often how little attention is paid nowadays to individualizing. No two persons are exactly alike, much less any two pupils. In vocal teaching, especially, it does great mischief to try to make one shoe fit every foot. I feel that those of my colleagues will agree with me, who, still possessing a thorough knowledge of the *Bel Canto*, have often undergone similar experiences. Yet the power of true vocal art, even in this decadent period, has lost but little of its effect on enthusiastic auditors. This is proved by the ever-renewed successes of Marcella Sembrich and others as contrasted with the great multitude of "natural" singers and dubious specialists with more or less voice. It is this fact, in particular, which encourages me to gather together the fruits of my experience in this little volume, for the benefit of my own pupils and other earnest vocal students. Let it be added, that this method has been tested by time, and that I can trace it back to the Italian singing-masters Gasparo Pacchierotti (d. 1821), Giovanni Battista Velluti (d. 1861), and others.

Should the technical information contained in these pages be found useful in wider circles, and do its part toward attracting and preserving many a talent to the service of the divine art of song, it would give the author the liveliest satisfaction.

G. B. LAMPERTI

BERLIN, 1905.

General Observations

The true method of singing is in harmony with nature and the laws of health.

Chief Requirements for the Pupil

Voice, musical talent, health, power of apprehension, diligence, and patience.

Chief Requirements for the Teacher

Experience, a sensitive ear, and the gift of intuition and individualization.

The Vocal Organs may be described briefly as "a pipe with double-reed, blown by means of diaphragm and lungs." The Voice results from the projection of an air-current against the Vocal Cords in varying degrees of tension. In forming the voice, three groups of muscles coöperate, namely, the Breathing-muscles, the Vocal muscles, and the Sound-modifying muscles.

The mode of breathing required for artistic singing is diaphragmatic breathing. It is the sole method by which a singer can conduct sufficient air tranquilly, and with a minimum of exertion, from the lungs to the vocal organs.*

---

* Prof. L. Mandl writes, in his "Hygiène de la voix," page 14, 2: "As long as the breathing is abdominal (diaphragmatic) no strain upon the vocal organs can proceed from the chest. . . . Neither will the larynx nor the pharynx be set in motion by the gentle breathing; everything remains at rest. After inspiration, therefore, the vocal organs are in a position to carry out properly, and without any hindrance that might otherwise have been caused by preceding contractions, the movements necessary to a slow expulsion of the air. Breath is taken easily through the wide-open glottis. . . ." Page 17, 5: "Singing-voices were preserved much better and longer by the old Italian method, as taught by Rubini, Porpora, etc., than by our modern methods, which teach (or at least permit) clavicular breathing. And those teachers who favor diaphragmatic breathing can likewise show the best results."

1. Diagram of the Action of the Diaphragm

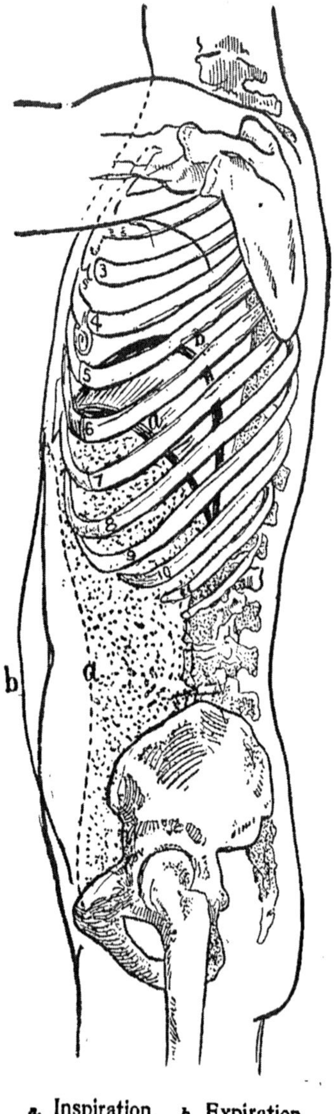

a. Inspiration. b. Expiration.

Preliminary Studies

(Vocal Gymnastics)

1. Position of the Body

The position of the body must be easy and natural. Throwing the weight on the right foot, which should be slightly advanced, let the pupil look straight ahead, much as if gazing on a picture, and in a wholly unconstrained posture; the expression of the face composed and pleasant, and the head erect, inclining neither forward nor backward. Take care, above all, that the muscles of neck and throat are not unnecessarily tense; the entire attitude must be easy and unconstrained. Hold the shoulder-joints free and loose, with the shoulders slightly thrown back to allow the chest due freedom in front, without raising it. For the present, the arms may hang loosely.

2. The Breathing

Before taking breath—which must be done at first only through the mouth, not through the nose—the mouth should be opened wide enough to permit the forefinger to pass between the upper and lower teeth (correct aperture -⊖-). Draw breath deeply, but quietly. We breathe *from* the lungs, but not *with* the lungs.*

---

*The principal breathing-muscle is the diaphragm, a muscular partition dividing the organs of the chest (lungs, heart) from the abdominal organs (liver, stomach, etc.). It is attached to the backbone, the lower ribs, and the front inner wall of the abdomen, and rises in the form of a dome to the height of the fourth rib. The act of breathing proceeds as follows: The muscular tissue of the diaphragm contracts, drawing the dome of the diaphragm downward, and forming in the lung-cavity above it a rarefied air-space, into which the air flows (passively) to counteract the atmospheric pressure. This is *Inspiration.*

By virtue of their own elasticity [and by reason of pressure from the expanded thorax], the lungs now seek to contract, thus exerting a slight pull on the depressed dome of the diaphragm; furthermore, the depressed abdominal organs are in a state of tension which strives for relaxation, due to pressure by the distended muscular walls of the abdomen and pelvis; and this combined pressure from above and below pushes up the dome of the diaphragm to the height of the fourth rib. This is *Expiration.*

It cannot be too strongly emphasized, that the diaphragm is the principal and essential breathing-muscle (if it should be crippled, breathing would cease and death ensue), and that Expiration is effected chiefly by the abdominal muscles. There are also so-called auxiliary breathing-muscles, those of the neck, back, and thorax, which may aid in sustaining an impaired breathing, but can never replace the regular function of the diaphragm. This shows that a sharp distinction between chest and abdominal breathing, such as was formerly generally accepted, cannot be maintained. Hence, our first endeavor must be to strengthen diaphragmatic breathing, and this can be accomplished only by systematically developing the abdominal muscles. It follows, that that part of the body in which the diaphragm must have freest play (from navel to breastbone, as viewed from outside), must in no way be hampered as to freedom of movement. The clothing should be made in conformity with this rule.

2. The Vocal Organs

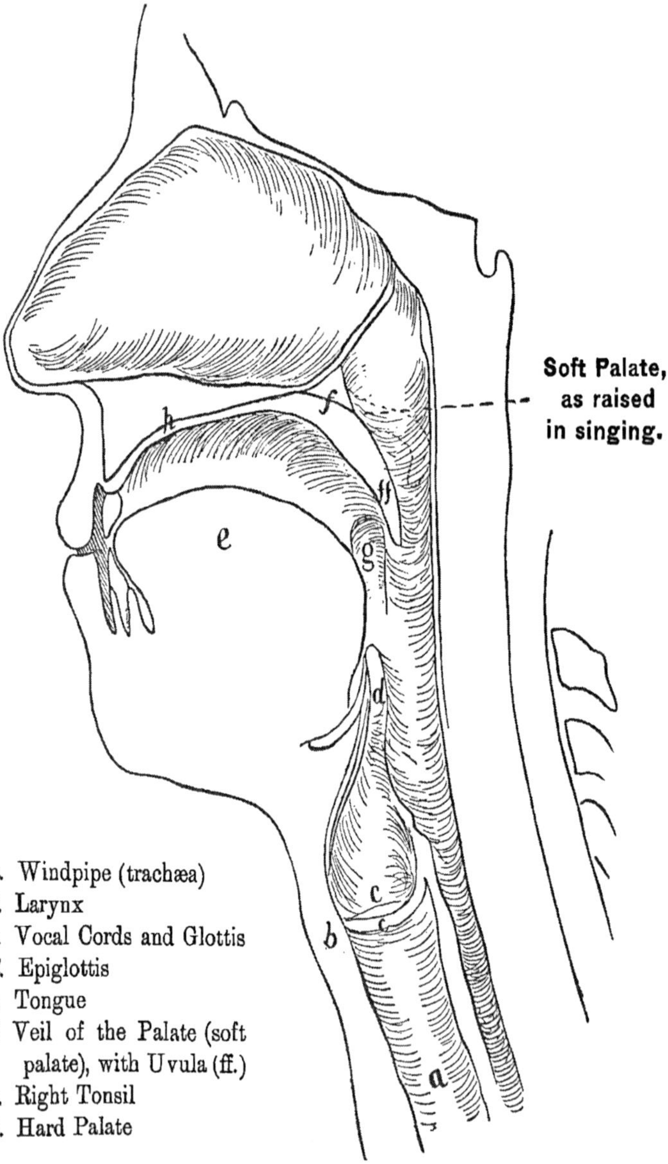

a. Windpipe (trachæa)
b. Larynx
c. Vocal Cords and Glottis
d. Epiglottis
e. Tongue
f. Veil of the Palate (soft palate), with Uvula (ff.)
g. Right Tonsil
h. Hard Palate

The cavities of the Pharynx, Chest and Head (mouth, nose, etc.) form the compound sounding-board of the vocal air-current.

The air drawn in (so to speak) in the form of a globular mass is now to be very gently and gradually expelled.* The Italian expression *filar il tuono*, "to spin out the tone," most aptly characterizes the required mode of expiration, which must proceed as naturally and unconstrainedly as the preceding inspiration. As long as it causes the pupil to feel any exertion, he has not acquired the right method. Note the time required for inspiration and expiration in seconds, and try to prolong this time gradually. When you have made, with due caution, some progress, repeat the exercise several times in succession, but not over ten times. Now try again to prolong the time of deep inspiration; in particular, the pause between inspiration and expiration, while holding the breath, should be prolonged as much as you can.

The act of tone-production is in "contrary motion" to that of breath-taking; the pull of the diaphragm goes parallel with the inspiration, whereas the push of the abdominal muscles is felt to oppose it (observe the movement of the abdominal walls), although both stand in causal conjunction. The breath-pressure increases regularly as the pitch in the tones rises. With insufficient pressure, the tone lacks in steadiness (*appoggio*; that is, the steady air-pressure on the vocal cords during tone-production). Higher breath-pressure presupposes deeper inspiration. Each and every tone must have steady support! The vocal point of support must be carefully distinguished from the points of resonance mentioned further on.

We think it advisable, at first, to attempt exercises in breathing, and later in tone-attack, only under the teacher's personal supervision; for just at this stage much harm may be done which is hard to undo afterwards. Reason: Breath-control is the foundation of all vocal study. It seems hardly necessary to warn against fatiguing the pupil.

As soon as the diaphragm functions as desired, and the rules for breathing have been taken to heart and rightly applied, the following Exercise may be taken up.

3. Tone-attack and Resonance

The tones proper for use in these exercises are the tones of the Medium Register. Let the pupil open his mouth as explained before, take breath, and sing with well-opened throat on the syllable "la," beginning on his comparatively best tone, between *piano* and *forte*. 

The tongue should be held as flat as possible, and must not arch upward. The *a* in *la* should

* The celebrated singing-master Velluti once warned a clergyman against a jerky style of speaking, as it would very soon cause hoarseness. All public speakers, and also officers, teachers, etc., should learn to speak naturally, that is, at the proper pitch and, above all things, drawing breath quietly and deeply, and never to overtax the voice.

sound like that in father.* Beauty and power of tone depend, not simply upon a correct tone-attack, but also on the resonance of the voice both in chest and head. With a well-opened throat, the tone should sound out steady, free and sonorous, like that of a violin or violoncello. One ought to feel the appoggio (point of support). Only a voice thus solidly founded will "carry," and always be plainly audible even in *pianissimo.* The point of aim for the tones of the Medium Register is the front of the hard palate.

Studies in Tone

The vocal registers are determined by the different points of resonance of the tones; † the mode of breathing always remains the same. There are three vocal registers, varying according to the individuality of the voice, namely, the Chest-, Medium, and Head-Register. A high, flexible female voice is termed a

Coloratura Soprano

and to this we shall now devote our attention. The Diatonic Major Scale gives us the best material for practice, because of the difficulty in taking the major Third, Sixth, and Seventh.‡

Exercise 1.

1. 

---

*In this very first exercise, the individual differences of the beginners will be manifest. Vocal ability and future success depend only too largely on the shape of the mouth and size of the tongue. The possessor of a broad, flat mouth can hardly ever learn to sing *piano.* We have our doubts concerning the success of a forcible training of the tongue by means of instruments, and the like. When the tip of the tongue curls up, there will always be trouble from this almost ineradicable defect. It is sometimes a good plan to begin with "le," as a preparation for the "ah" with a normal position of the tongue. Take care that the larynx (carryiug the vocal cords) does not rise unnaturally high while singing; otherwise the tone will sound "throaty," from the narrowing of the vocal tube. Mechanical and grammatical faults of speech must be overcome. The injurious "stroke of the glottis" should under no consideration be employed in tone-attack; it ruins the voice, and ought, in spite of the apparent certainty attained in tone-production, to be wholly eschewed.

† To determine the natural registers of any voice requires the experience and acute ear of the teacher. In this particular many an ill deed is done. The capability of vocalizing on high tones affords a clew of some value. Some coloratura sopranos have no developed chest-register.

‡ The minor Third is easier to take than the major, which accounts for the prominence of the minor mode in Folk-music.

The singer, while attentive to her voice, should observe in a mirror the opening of the mouth and expression of the face; but she must sing out into the room, not against the wall.

Remark for the Teacher. The teacher must decide on which tone in the medium register the lesson shall begin. He should neither sing with the pupil, nor accompany her on the piano with the tone she is singing. As a matter of course, only a well-tuned instrument ought to be used. Only when the pupil feels uncertain, should the teacher sing to her, and support her with the piano in unison. He should also show her the proper posture of the mouth, and breathe with her, though without singing. It is remarkable what an important rôle suggestive action plays in vocal instruction. Nervous clearing of the throat between the exercises should be peremptorily forbidden. Pay special attention to the opening of the mouth, to the tongue, and to the facial expression. Here the old saying is applicable, "The eye is the mirror of the soul." The pupil must also avoid a listening attitude while singing, because it tends to stiffen the muscles of the throat.

Binding of two tones (*legato*).

2. 

The following tone must be bound closely to the first, much as in piano-playing, when the first finger must not be lifted till the second one strikes. Therefore, do not sing the tones detatched! (.......) This exercise is also to be sung only *mf*, nearly *p*; and the rules already given must be strictly observed.

Exercises for Steadying the Vocal Attack

1. Piano. 

In the above exercises, observe a strict *legato*, a smooth and unbroken passage from one tone to the other. The breathing must not be interrupted between the tones, but flow on evenly as if a single tone were to be sung. At the close of each exercise or phrase, a comfortable amount of air must remain in the lungs; for it is a vicious and injurious habit to finish a passage with exhausted lungs. Remember, that no small part of the artistic effect sought by the vocalist depends upon a correct close; at the close one should be in the same physical attitude as if one intended to continue singing. We have already briefly remarked, that in passing from low tones to higher ones the breathing must proceed in a contrary sense: The higher the tones, the deeper the breathing!

Vocal Development, and Blending of the Registers

(Compare Observations on Change of Register, page 23.)

The ascending tones *c e g c* in Ex. (a) are to be sung *legato*. The teacher may sing *to* the pupil, but never *with* her.

After c^2 take only a short breath, and return in *portamento*-style to low c^1. The time-value of a note after which one takes breath (in this case c^2) will be slightly abbreviated, but in such a manner as not to be perceptible to the listener. While taking breath the mouth must not be closed. A student with plenty of breath may even sing the whole exercise in one breath. Above all things, see that the position of the mouth is correct, and that it readily and naturally adapts itself to each successive higher tone.

On high *d♭* (Ex. b) a change of register will usually occur.* Here begins the head-voice, so called because the point of resonance is felt in the head. Let the pupil try to sing *d♭-f-a♭-d♭*. On high *d♭* the lower jaw must sink somewhat further than in the medium register, and the resonance of the tone should be distinctly felt in the top of the head near the front, but not in the forehead or in the back of the head. To make this point plainer, let the pupil sing high *d♭* on "li" (lee), with a short pause before taking the head-tone. The mouth-opening will become slightly rounded, the vowel shaded towards "o." In the first half of the exercise, the *legato* must on no account be changed into a dragging-over of one tone into the other.

N.B. If the skip of a Fourth makes this exercise too difficult—particularly for a weak medium register and short breath—let the following exercise precede it:

(c) 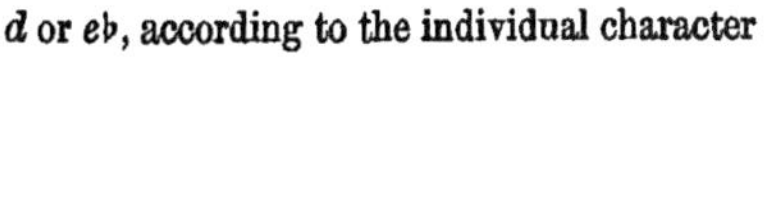

*Sometimes not till *d* or *e♭*, according to the individual character of the voice.

In order to bind the tones well, to keep the breathing quiet, and (later) to blend the registers properly, the following exercise will serve:

(d) 

N.B. At this stage we would call attention to the correct manner of taking breath. Never take breath at the bar, but after the strong beat of the next measure.

The high c^2, marked with a fermata 𝄐, must glide into and die away on *b*. A change of register occurs on $c^2\sharp$. In these exercises one should never reach the extreme limit of the vocal range; for this reason the note f^2 was assumed as highest tone, which need not be taken as a standing rule for all cases.

Some beginners find the next exercise more difficult than those preceding, especially when the breathing is not under full control. In such cases, skip to the exercise following it.

N.B. Do not fail to note the change of register here! (Though in some voices it may not occur till *d*.)

Do not forget that breathing and voice-production are in "contrary motion." While the teacher is singing the pupil should feel, by applying the palm of the hand, how the "air-press" works.

In the last exercise, the head-tone will "speak" more readily if aided by a slight extra-pressure, and it is also allowable to draw a little breath through the nose. As we said before, the resonance must be felt on top of the head, about where the parietal bone joins the frontal bone (frontoparietal suture).

The following remark is highly important, and the pupil should give it serious attention: It is a vicious fault to let the tone break off abruptly at the close, which happens when one fails to have breath in reserve and to remain with open mouth in the same posture. As a continual reminder of this fault we shall use the following small note appended to the full melody-note, to indicate unmistakably the proper time for the close.

Exercise 4 is to be sung in one breath. Head-tones are indicated by square notes. How high the progressive transposition can extend, depends on skilfulness and vocal quality,—seldom above *eb*. On notes marked with an exclamation-point, look out for pure intonation!

Vocal Agility (Coloratura)

It is an important matter to train the voice in flexibility. Even voices which are naturally rebellious and heavy are sure to gain by it in mellowness and beauty. When the training is insufficient, coloratura-passages are often slurred over, or delivered jerkily (*cavallina*). Each individual tone must sound full and round. This, however, will be the case only when the singer's delivery combines the *legato* with the *détaché*—when her tone-production is at once well-supported and light. The mode of breathing remains unchanged; even in rapid passages no essential alteration in the bodily attitude and so forth should occur. The above-noted style of tone-production might most aptly be termed *sostenuto*, a style which excludes from the outset the so-called "bleating" tone. Coloratura-passages must be sung strictly in time, and never rapidly, but rather slowly.* When the pupil has no natural gift, do not waste time on coloratura study.

1a

Before beginning to practise the above Exercise, the intonation of the difficult intervals should be established; practise them with intentional emphasis. When singing the remaining tones, pitch them with reference to the starting-tone (keynote) marked ⊕. Assume low *c* as a point of rest, from which the following tones proceed in ever-widening circles; or imagine a ball bounding from the ground in regularly increasing leaps. No *legato!* the following Exercise is to be sung *sostenuto!*

b.

The high *g* forms the point of departure whence the other tones are pitched. The first half of the exercise is preparatory; the second should be sung *piano.*

2.

* Avoid marking time with head, hands, or feet.

la
rit.
to F
3.
rit.
Allegretto.
la
4.
Moderato.
la
5.
Allegro vivace.
la
6.

N.B. When the singer has plenty of breath, the breathing-marks may be disregarded.

The Trill

The art of repeating two neighboring tones in rapid alternation presupposes natural gifts; otherwise skill can be attained only very gradually by dint of great diligence and perseverance. The principal note takes the accent, the auxiliary follows lightly. Trill-practice is excellent for pure intonation. At first practise slowly, but always strictly in time; before proficiency is reached, no *accelerando* should be attempted. Not every voice is suited for this embellishment; heavy voices may even be injured by purposeless trill-practice. In singing, begin on the harmonic principal note.

Preparation and Acceleration of the Trill

(Intonation!)

Trills Without Preparation (Shakes)

Turns.

Chromatic Scales

(Pure Intonation !)

Detached Tones : Staccato

Staccato-practice must be very cautiously proceeded with. In contrast with the preceding *marcato*, the tones are now executed short, as indicated by dots or short dashes over the notes. When the pupil shows no natural aptitude for this vocal style the short *staccato* should not be practised too frequently, as it might easily injure the voice. First of all, the head-resonance must come into action. A slight extra-pressure, but without waste of breath, makes the tone "speak" easily. Notes marked with *staccato*-dots lose half their time-value; those marked with wedge-shaped dashes lose about three-quarters.

Sustained Tones, and the Messa di Voce

Not until the voice has gained decided agility and facility, should the pupil begin to practise sustained tones, together with the *Messa di voce* (the long, even *crescendo* and *decrescendo*). Practise strictly in time, on the vowel "ah," beginning very *piano* and letting the tone swell gradually to *forte*. Take care that no interruption or abrupt increase occurs in the smooth swell:

not  still less  or 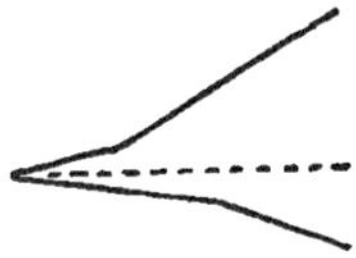

While we have hitherto aimed at bringing the tone as far forward as possible, we must now carry it further back toward the pharynx. The diaphragm must work easily and elastically, like India rubber, letting the air stream out gently. The *Messa di voce* is produced solely by breath-control. The spinning-out of the tone (*filare la voce*) is very difficult; it must be managed with the utmost circumspection, and not attempted at all until now. In the *decrescendo* the breath-pressure decreases very gradually and evenly, thus:

Always think of the tone of a violin. The *piano*—as it were the daughter, not the shadow, of the *forte*—must float lightly on the lips; hence the saying, *cantare a fior di labbra.*

At the close the breath should not be exhausted, but should be suitably graduated and husbanded. Moreover, one ought to be able to sustain a tone eighteen or twenty seconds.

The Portamento

Portamento (from *portare,* to carry) signifies the gentle carrying-over (not dragging-over) of one tone to another. In doing so, the second tone is barely audibly anticipated at the end of the first. The voice describes, so to speak, an upward or downward curve, while the *appoggio* remains unmoved.

When voice and breathing act in the same direction, and the *appoggio* (point of support) is abandoned, the result is an awkward drawl, or (if taken slower) a long-drawn howl, a very common fault; do not sing thus: 

The opposite of the *portamento* (which adds great charm to the style, if not too often employed) is the Direct Attack of the higher or lower tone (*di slancio*, or *di posto*).

Special studies for the *portamento* are not required here, because sufficient opportunity will be found, in the solfeggi and vocalises, for upward or downward *portamenti*, as indicated by the *legato*-slur. The wider the interval, the more difficult the execution. Refined taste is essential to the proper employment of this vocal device.

Remark for the Teacher. No more exercises will be needed, if the pupil shows ability. In fact, less depends on the exercises themselves than on the manner in which they are practised and applied. Useless fatigue and discouragement can certainly not lead to success in study.

Female Voices

Coloratura Soprano

Dramatic Soprano (or High Mezzo-Soprano)

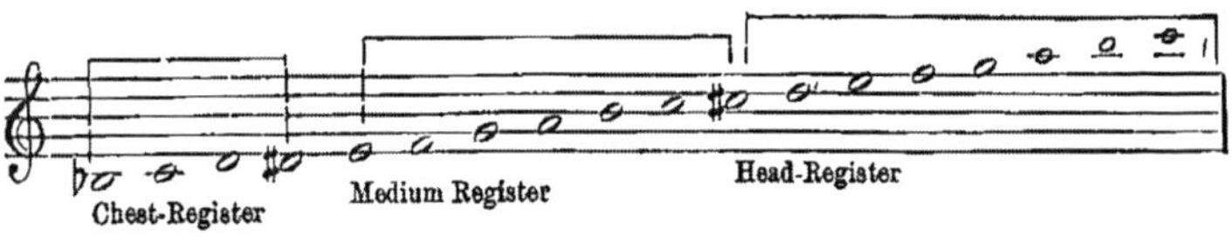

The Mezzo-Soprano, also called Dramatic Soprano, is a less flexible female voice with developed chest-register and medium compass. The course of study is nearly the same as for the coloratura soprano; it begins by developing the medium register, adding later the higher and lower tones. How many of the preceding exercises should be practised, depends wholly upon the character of the voice and the pupil's talent.

Observations on Change of Register

It often happens, on again hearing a beautiful voice after the lapse of years, that we are astonished at its loss of sonority and mellowness; changes of register are plainly audible; the voice is apt to break, and no longer follows the artistic intentions. The cause may generally be traced to wrong development and treatment. For instance, if the chest-register be forced up unnaturally, the voice must necessarily suffer. A given voice should not be classified simply according to its actual compass, but also according to its *timbre*. As for the correct employment of the registers, general rules can hardly be formulated. There are female voices, for example, in which the registers are naturally blended, that is, in which the unbiassed listener scarcely notices the passage from one to the other. Where this is not the case, the teacher must continue training until the pupil is able to blend the registers smoothly. Should the ear, however, be unable to distinguish the difference in tone-effect, it argues a defective natural talent in the pupil. The tones near to the change of register must always be taken with great care. Sing *e-f-g* slowly, on *la*. As the chest-voice (of a mezzo-soprano) passes over into the medium register, although the character or *timbre* of the tone must naturally change, yet the volume and general effect of the tone should remain the same; in other words, the tones should be so evenly matched that the balance of tone is held level from the lowest to the highest note of the scale. Even eminent vocalists often sing impure, flat head-tones at the end of a passage ascending from the lower register. This results from a weakness of the diaphragm, which is unable to support the tone by full pressure. There is no doubt that the greater part of the difficulties encountered at a change of register, as well as the uneven tones within one and the same register, may be traced to faulty breathing. At a change of register, especially, the breathing must be calm and easy. When it is so, and when the body is in a normal position, with mouth and pharynx suitably opened, no one will experience difficulty at a change of register. Curiously enough, teachers are still to be found who simply allow the solfeggi to be transposed, instead of making due allowance for the differences of register in different kinds of voices. In such cases one need not be surprised to hear of vocal defects which cannot result when the voice is naturally developed.—Therefore, first of all, learn to breathe correctly!

Following the exercises, solfeggi are now to be studied. To acquire a pure pronunciation of the vowels, always practise on *do re mi fa sol la si*, observing the rules given below:

1. For the vowels *a*, *e*, *i*, open the mouth about a fingerbreadth.
2. For *o*, the lips should assume an only slightly rounded form.
3. In the medium register, tones on the vowels *e* and *i* should be felt

near the front of the hard palate; the tones of the head-register should be felt to vibrate in the top of the skull, near the front.

4. Pronounce the consonant *s* sharply in *sol* and *si.*

5. Two successive consonants, ending one word and beginning the next, must be sung separately; for instance, *sol, la,* not *solla.*

A class of voice becoming more and more rare is the Contralto, or Alto. What is nowadays usually understood as alto, was formerly termed a deep mezzo-soprano. The modern opera-repertory seldom affords opportunity for a genuine deep alto to participate: and present-day composers, though they may write for this voice, pay little attention to its compass and peculiarities. Small wonder, then, that our altos are gradually being converted into mezzo-sopranos!

For the sake of brevity we shall discuss both these classes (high and low alto) under the head of

Deep Female Voices

The beauty of a low voice resides in the chest-register, with the development of which one ought to begin, the medium and head-registers following. In low voices the medium register is very weak, and requires special care for its proper development. The low and high "border-tones" are not to be added till later. At first, the main point is considered to be chest-resonance, with a well-opened pharynx. An alto voice without sufficient *appoggio* does not carry, and sounds dull and hollow. (Compare "Tone-attack and Resonance," on page 9.) Approach the development of the high tones only with the utmost caution. When the chest-voice is forced up too high, the head-voice loses in mellowness and carrying-power; how many beautiful alto voices have been ruined—caused to break—by this unnatural method! The diagram given above shows quite accurately the relations of the various registers. In case a deep alto has no natural gift for coloratura, do not try to force its inclination unnecessarily, for such purposeless practice may easily lead to forcing the voice and acquiring the *tremolo.* It is a different matter with the high alto, which often has a natural talent for coloratura, whence it is called "coloratura alto" in contradistinction to "dramatic alto."

Alto singers are not seldom inclined to pronounce the "ah" like "oh"; a defect which should be contended against from the very first exercises on the attack.

In general, the rules already given should be observed.

After sufficient preparation (position of the body, breathing, and attack) similar vocal studies are to be taken up as for soprano.

Male Voices

From anatomic reasons (larger pharynx and longer vocal cords) male voices sound an octave lower than female voices. Through mutation the boy's voice, which much resembles the female voice, becomes either a high or a deep male voice.

High Male Voices:

Tenor (Heroic, Lyric, and Light Tenor).

Deep Male Voices:

Baritone (Bass- and Tenor-Baritone).
Bass (deep and high; the latter is the *buffo*).

One of these classes, too, the genuine baritone (not to be confounded with the high bass) is gradually disappearing for certain reasons. As a typical baritone we would name Giorgio Ronconi, for whom Donizetti wrote operatic rôles. The light tenors, too, are being gradually superseded by the heroic tenor.

Besides the registers already enumerated (chest, medium, and head), the male voice possesses a fourth, which renders it essentially different from the female voice, namely, the "mixed voice" (*voix mixte*), wrongly called "falsetto." And the very fact that the training of this register has been neglected, may be the chief reason that we have so few eminent tenors, and that artists endowed with great vocal powers often mistake *quantity* of tone for *quality*. How few singers there are who can sing with "half-breath"; how few who know how to control or employ the *messa di voce* or an effective, buoyant *piano!* And may not this be attributed to faulty methods of breathing?

Tenor

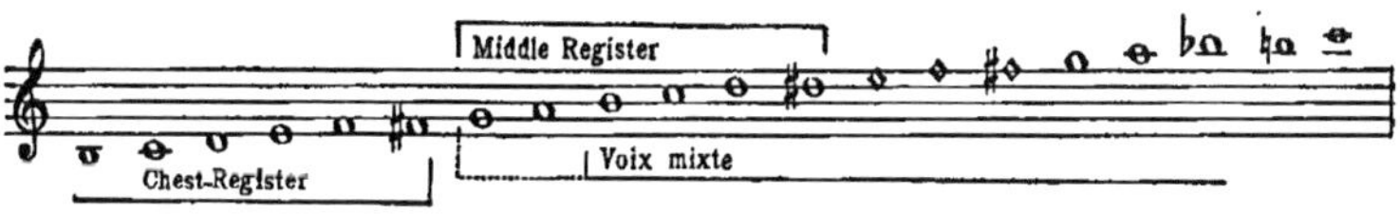

The proper cultivation of a tenor voice requires great experience, and forms the most difficult task for the singing-teacher. On the tones *b*, *c*, *d*, and *d*♯

head-resonance mingles with the chest-voice carried on from below,* so that the singer sings with but half the chest-resonance. The main point is, to blend the medium register with the so-called *voix mixte;* the chief object to keep in view being to acquire an even scale from the lowest tone to the highest.

We begin, as with the soprano, with developing the medium register, which is the only possible foundation for a healthful and natural high register. Let the pupil sing the tone deep *d* on "la" (*lah*), but without sustaining it, and proceed upward to *g*, thus:

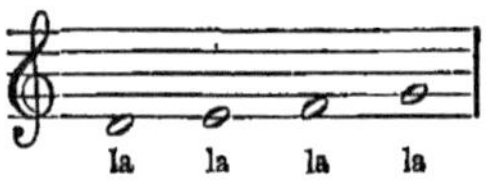

Upon this tone the exercises for the attack should commence. Everything which we have previously said about the breathing (see page 7) must be reviewed at this point. Indeed, for the tenor voice we would make the former rules still more stringent; perfect breath-control is far more important for this class of voice than for any other. After all, what is Song but expanded Speech, in which the breathing proceeds quietly and with continuous regularity? The point of resonance for the medium voice is the hard palate; for the head-tones, the top of the head, in front. Should the latter vibrate in the forehead, the high tones will lack metallic resonance. Sing *mezza voce*, and be careful not to force the medium register. Regarding the beauty of the tone, we must now, unfortunately, in contrast with former times, strive to reproduce the ideal tone of violinist and violoncellist; whereas these latter used to imitate the tones of great singers. The tones of the tenor voice should resemble the high tones of the violoncello, in that one cannot hear, contrasting them with violin-tones, that they are 16-foot tones, that is, that they sound an octave lower. Our former observations on the Attack are to be reviewed (p. 9). Special faults, which ought not to arise when tone-production and breathing are correct, and the body held properly, are the following:

1. Insufficient chest-resonance produces a flat tone without carrying-power; the voice seems to hang in the air.
2. When the pharynx is too widely opened, the tone sounds hollow.
3. Rigidity of the throat-muscles causes a "choked" tone.
4. When the tongue is held wrong, the tone is guttural.
5. When the larynx is held too high, the pharynx is unduly contracted, and the so-called "throaty" tone results.
6. Too much nasal resonance renders the tone nasal (wrong point of resonance; veil of the palate not raised!).

---

* In the case of "light" tenors the *voix mixte* often begins still lower.

7. When the mouth is not opened wide enough, the "dental" tone results from the tonal resonance on the teeth.

8. Weakness of the laryngeal muscles and vocal cords may cause the *tremolo*. Therefore, one should spare the voice and not sing with full force.

When a good *appoggio* is acquired, and the voice "speaks" to the teacher's satisfaction, the following studies may be taken up; sing them at first on "la" (*lah*), and then on "le" (*lay*, like the French *lé*; acute *é*, not broad *è*). The most difficult tones for the tenor voice are

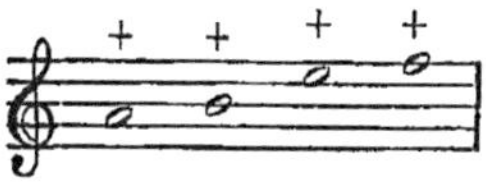

la, *si* and *mi*, *fa*. Wherever they occur, give them especial attention.

The course of study is the same as for Soprano, only the trill-exercises may be omitted. We consider this an undignified embellishment for a man's voice, and reject its use from the standpoint of musical æsthetics. Our observations on the soprano course remain in force here.

1.

2.

3.

4.

5. 

6. 

We would remark, finally, that all controversies and disputes touching the development of the tenor voice are usually quite pointless, for the simple reason that nothing more can be made of any given voice, when naturally trained and developed, than the given anatomical conditions permit. No method whatever will ever succeed in making something great out of every voice, for that would certainly be unnatural—contrary to nature. What, then, is the singing-teacher's chief problem? Let us take the Italian terms, for once: *Posare* (*appoggiare*), *sviluppare*, *eguagliare la voce* (to place, develop, and equalize the voice). These are now and always the fundamental ideas of the technics of the *bel canto.* And everybody ought to learn to sing according to correct methods, at least, so as to develop the muscles employed in singing; which is also to be warmly recommended from a hygienic point of view, more particularly for persons having weak lungs.

The remaining classes of voice, Baritone and Bass, we shall include under the head of

Deep Male Voices

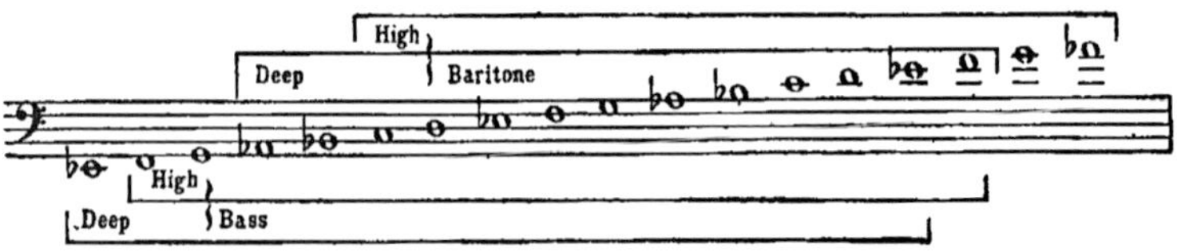

The above diagram exhibits the usual compass of these voices.

The Baritone is considered the typical male voice. Its very name indicates this—*barytonos*=deep-sounding. We have already remarked that this class of voice is undergoing a gradual process of lowering. Its ordinary compass is from A to $f'\sharp$:

In vocalizing the tones *c*, *d*, *e*, sing them with breadth of tone, but *not* on broad *a* (law). The medium register starts on $f\sharp$; keep the pharynx well opened. High *e* is the limit of the head-register; beginning about on c', the half chest-resonance is reinforced by head-resonance. The change of register must be equalized beforehand. A good *appoggio*, more especially when the chest-register has first been developed, insures strong high tones. High e' should be sung broadly, but rather darkly.

The development of the High Bass calls for no special observations.

The tones of the medium register are to be sung with an open, somewhat round *ah.*

The Deep Bass (*basso profondo*) differs from the high bass, as the deep alto from the high, by greater breadth and sonority of the low tones. Be very careful not to force the chest-register up too high. The difficulty in making the lowest tones "speak" tires the voice, and for this reason a careful development of the medium register should be aimed at.

The Technics of Speech and Song

Language and Song rarely go hand in hand. The Italian language is the chief exception to this rule, being the one best adapted for artistic song on account of its wealth of vowels and lack of aspirates. Most Italians naturally pronounce the open vowel "a" (ah) correctly, whereas other nationalities have to make a special study of it; the English, for instance, often shade "ah" toward *a* or *o*. For us, however, the German language is the first in order. The vowels "i" (ee) and French "u" (ü) are hard to sing on the high notes. We shall take no singer to task for changing the position of such words, or for substituting others with more euphonious vowels—provided that he possess the technical ability to vocalize the above-named vowels on high tones. The pronunciation of the vowels having been sufficiently practised in the solfeggi and vocalises, we need dwell no longer on their quantity (as long or short); for a pure pronunciation, free from dialect and sharply articulated, is a prerequisite.

We proceed to the German diphthongs, pronounced as follows:

ai and ei = ah[i]
äu and eu = ah[ü]
au = ah[oo]

The first vowel must be prolonged as much as possible, and the second sung short.

The pronunciation of the consonants presents greater difficulties than that of the vowels. Consonants are vocal or unvocal. The vocal nasal consonants (*m*, *n*, *ng*) require no special remark. Opinions differ concerning the correct pronunciation of *g* at the end of a word or syllable. In the words *König* and *heilig*, the soft sound of *g* (the German palatal *ch*) is preferable; on the other hand, we pronounce *weg* like *weck*, *sag* like *sak* (*zahk*), although we say *wech*-genommen (not *weck*genommen) because of the two successive *g*'s. The consonants *h* and *ch* are peculiar to the German language, and therefore familiar to all.* Far more unfavorable for vocal art are the numerous doubled consonants and combinations. The tone-accent always falls on the vowel; *e. g.*, pronounce *Hi-mmel*, not *Him-mel*. Where no ambiguity is created the final and initial consonants may be drawn together, *e. g.*, "im⁀milden Mondlicht" (English parallel: "in⁀noble hearts"); but make a distinction between "in Nacht" and "in Acht" (parallel: "a tall" and "at all"). Some sentences are so crowded with combinations of consonants as positively to hinder the freedom of delivery. The best way to overcome such difficult word-complexes is, to try to treat entire sentences like one word, to dwell on the vowels, and to glide lightly over the consonants, though without becoming indistinct. In extreme emotion the voice is sometimes intentionally modulated into a speaking tone, as when Fidelio exclaims, in the scene in the subterranean prison, "Töt' erst sein Weib!" (first kill his wife). The same likewise occurs in songs and ballads, or in any sharply and passionately declaimed passages.

Some Remarks on Musical Style

No one has as yet asserted his ability to teach the correct interpretation of music, although attempts have been made, especially of late years, to deduce

---

*For English-speaking students unacquainted with German, an explanation appears desirable: The hard, or guttural, *ch* is merely a rough breathing, as if one were trying gently to clear one's throat; the soft, or palatal, *ch* is obtained by setting the tongue as if to pronounce "ye," and then, *retaining the tongue in that position*, breathing (whispering) "he" through between tongue and hard palate.—TRANSLATOR'S NOTE.

rules of universal application from interpretations inspired by musical feeling and refined taste. As a noteworthy essay on this subject we would recommend Lussy's "Kunst des musikalischen Vortrags" (Art of Musical Interpretation), published by Leuckart, Leipzig—*a work which stimulates independent thinking about music which one hears. Innate talent, however, must be seconded by another gift—artistic taste, which is most clearly exhibited in the dynamics (tone-power) and correct tempo (instinct for time). Compositions of olden times are often played too fast; even as early as 1752 Quantz, in his "Essay on Playing the German Flute," makes the same observation. Especially in works by the old masters, with rare indications of the tempo, one should guard against a too-hurried *allegro.* Everything written about the embellishments of those days, has failed to settle the questions involved. Artistic taste is a greater help than interesting historical discussions. Many an old vocal grace, like certain forms of the trill, and the rapid repetition of one tone (compare Caccini, 1601), has become totally obsolete.

Correct musical accentuation depends, firstly, on the rhythmic phrasing, and secondly, on tone-accent and word-accent. Here the general theory of music steps in; the theory of the strong and weak beat, of consonance and dissonance, and of metrics. For a good style the art of correct phrasing is of the highest importance. Phrasing is simply musical punctuation, which frequently coincides with that of the words. The shading, or musical *nuances,* of a phrase will depend on tempo and general character of the composition. Although sentences should never be torn asunder by thoughtless breathing, there are times, nevertheless, when one is obliged to take breath before a new word. It is never permissible to separate the conjunction "and" from a following sentence which it joins to what precedes; breath must be taken beforehand.

In the Recitative (from *recitare,* to narrate), singing most nearly approaches ordinary speech. The chief requirement for this vocal style is, that the singer's imagination should be fired by the given situation. One of its forms, the so-called *recitativo secco,* with a rather sketchy chord-accompaniment, was formerly employed to hasten the course of the dramatic action, and as a means of joining the principal numbers of the opera, or to put the epic (narrative) element in musical shape, more especially for narrating previous occurrences. It represents the light and easy conversational tone of everyday life. What an evolution, that of this simple musical form into the recitatives of a Verdi, and yet more into the recitative-style of Richard Wagner, in which tone-accent and word-accent coincide and blend in a manner unknown before! In the Wagner drama the vocal part is wrought into a symphonic tissue of tone, and only a singer with a perfectly trained voice can satisfy the demands of the musical

* The latest Paris edition (1904) is entitled "Traité de l'expression musicale."

declamation. Richard Wagner, himself, writes on vocal technics as follows: "It is certain that in no other study is such assiduous individual attention required, as in singing-lessons. It demands ever-vigilant supervision of the least details, and unwearying patience in most arduous practice, to acquire a really faultless development of the human voice, particularly in Germany under the influence of the German language. Whereas, in learning all instruments the laws of their technics rest on a firm foundation, and may be taught the student, in accordance with fixed rules, by any thoroughly trained executant on a given instrument, the technics of vocal art are to this day an unsolved problem. Simply our observation of the fact, that the theory of singing has not been taught with genuine success in a single German Conservatory, is sufficient evidence of this difficulty."*

After finishing the most important vocal exercises, the student may begin the study of light Arias; for example:

For Coloratura Soprano:	*La Sonnambula, Le Nozze di Figaro*
Dramatic Soprano:	*Otello* (Rossini), *Semiramide*
{ Mezzo-Soprano:	*La Favorita*
{ High Alto:	*Don Sebastiano* (Donizetti)
Low Alto:	*L'Italiana in Algeri*
Light Tenor:	*I Puritani* (Bellini)
Lyric Tenor:	*Lucia di Lammermoor*
Dramatic Tenor:	*Poliuto* (Donizetti), *Il Profeta*
Baritone:	*Maria di Rohan* (Donizetti) and *Il Barbiere di Siviglia*
High Bass:	*Semiramide* (Rossini)
Low Bass:	*Roberto il Diavolo*

Regarding them as studies, all arias are to be sung in Italian; the more difficult languages will be considered later. The first step is, to ascertain the prevailing mood to be interpreted, according to which the tempo and style can then be determined. The singer must clearly understand what the poem expresses, before undertaking serious study of the melody. What poet and composer felt while creating the composition, must be felt (or, better, *re-created*) by the singer. No interpretation can rightly be called perfect until the poetical and musical conception is exhaustively set forth; until the hearer, carried away by the artistic effect, forgets the artist in rapt contemplation of the art-work. —Breathing and phrasing must be settled, and all expression-marks carefully noted.

The Arioso and the Song make still higher demands on the artistic capacity. The modern German *Lied*, in particular, presupposes great technical

* "Collected Writings," vol. viii, p. 199.

skill and powers of interpretation to render it effective, not merely by potent characterization and fervor of style, but also from a purely musical viewpoint.* Powerful declamation cannot make up, in the long run, for defective tone-production and ill-traced melodic lines. Were it otherwise, how sad for pure vocal art, which should find in the concert-hall, divorced from the actualities of the dramatic stage, a field for fresh triumphs!

Now, how should a Song ("Lied") be studied? Read through the poem carefully, and make mental note of its content. Then play the melody through slowly. Specially difficult intervals must be strongly impressed on the ear. It is a good plan to pass over gradually from the speaking-tone to the singing-tone. During this time the Song emerges in nebulous contours before the student's fancy. When the expression-marks are observed, its form grows clearer and clearer until, the accompaniment being added, it gains its true *coloris* and a well-defined shape. By dint of singing dubious passages over and over, with a decided interval between the repetitions, distinctness and confidence are obtained. And, finally, what we have learned has to be memorized. The singer is not invariably obliged to follow the composer's intimations exactly; take, for example, the passage in "Die beiden Grenadiere" by Schumann, "So will ich liegen und horchen still, wie eine Schildwach' im Grabe," for which *forte* is directed. But such cases are exceptional; as a rule the author's written instructions should be held by the pupil as most precious suggestions.

A Word on the Study of Rôles

The versatility demanded of our modern stage-singers excludes, to a certain extent, the possibility of their attaining real eminence in any one direction. What an amount of diligence and energy is required merely for mastering the repertory of a court theatre! Formerly it was different; the singer sang few rôles, and those only for which he was adapted. Nowadays it may happen, that to-day a coloratura soprano has to sing Rosine, to-morrow Mignon, and the day after one of the Valkyries. This is not simply frivolous, but a sin against the spirit of art. Liberally endowed theatres should strictly define the various character-specialties, and spare the voices. There is no lack of vocal talent; but the conditions of modern art are unfavorable to orderly development. The singer does not study long enough, begins his stage-career unripe, and very seldom indeed grows up into the "great" rôles. And besides, there is the fairly overwhelming crop of mediocrity, forced in music-schools of every degree,

* We warn students against too much *Lied*-singing at first, the range being too limited and the numerous tone-repetitions calculated to tire the voice; coloratura sopranos, in particular, should take this warning to heart.

beleaguering the Director's door! Many a highly promising talent falls a victim to such competition, and prefers a private life to this hurry and worry.—But to return to our subject: How should one study an operatic rôle? Whoever would be an opera-singer, should early gain familiarity with the stage. After finishing, or even during, his vocal course, he must learn the elements of the mimic art, and take lessons in acting. While studying a rôle, the dramatic connection is important for correctly grasping its meaning. First of all, the climax of the action ought to be critically examined, for all secondary situations follow as a matter of course. Much practice tires the voice; it is therefore better merely to mark the tones lightly. In former times the singers were less lavish of their vocal material, than now; the less important passages were slighted, so that at critical moments they might be in full possession of their voices. Indeed, this style more nearly approaches nature; for no one, in every-day life, always speaks pathetically with a raised voice. However, singing *mezza voce* fatigues beginners in practising. It is more important to learn with the head, without using the voice. It is a great advantage to know how to study, that is, without tiring oneself. Whistling the melody makes the throat dry. It is not a good plan to hum the part an octave lower, or to transpose it for the sake of facility. Some modern conductors tire the singers out by keeping time too strictly. It is precisely in free delivery, in "*tempo rubato*," that a great artist makes his effect, and more particularly in Italian music. Although the Pasta sang Norma according to Bellini's intentions, it was the Malibran who first made the well-known terzetto "Oh! di qual sei tu vittima" grandly effective, and this by following her own ideas quite regardless of the composer's. Frequent practice is of more use than long, wearisome rehearsals. The singer should become absorbed in the character of his rôle, and practise before a mirror: Keep the head cool, the heart warm! Through over-devotion to the comparatively mechanical "business" of the hands, the expression of the eyes, "the mirror of the soul," is often neglected. Distinct enunciation, pointed declamation, and a striking impersonation of the character enacted, are the chief requisites for the modern music-drama. Not merely seething blood and vulgar ranting, but, above all things, deep feeling! * At this point, when the artist's entire individuality is taxed, there is no time left to repair defects of vocal technique; the singer must now learn to set forth, in the focus of the dramatic movement on the stage, what he has already acquired. A beautiful voice without emotional power is like a lovely woman without wit.

Care of the Voice. Hygiene

If you would keep your voice fresh and vigorous, do not ask more of it

*Particularly for singing in Italian, "aspiration" is held to be a valuable technical device for increasing the intensity of emotional expression.

than it can bear! A natural method strengthens the body and the vocal organ; the singer himself must now be careful to avoid everything which might affect his voice injuriously. A strong, thoroughly trained organ will by no means, as many erroneously think, be ruined by Wagner's music; the fatal mistake is rather, that unripe artists undertake the most difficult tasks before possessing the necessary ability. And even a singer with but a small voice, and obliged to limit himself to a narrow range, ought to make an intelligent selection from among these few rôles. Too much song-singing, as we said before, is harmful. Besides, special hygienic directions should be followed. We would refer to the before-mentioned work by Professor Dr. Mandl (German title: "Gesundheitslehre der Stimme"), which gives most excellent advice, even for minor indispositions. Space forbids our entering into all details. We warn the singer against unnecessarily loud speaking, especially in the more important rôles. One ought not to sing soon after eating; and it is injurious to eat much butter or fatty food in general. Practising with moderation, and with frequent interruptions, we have already advised. For the rest, one should lead a well-regulated life, and avoid whatever might affect the system injuriously. For the same reason, one should stop singing entirely during indisposition, and allow the vocal organ to rest. Avoid, above all, sudden changes of temperature, which may easily give rise to catarrh, whose unpleasant effects should not be underestimated by a vocal artist, of all persons. "Coddling," on the other hand, opens every avenue to disease; one should rather seek refuge in hardening the system. Breathing through the nose in the open air, and an avoidance of overheating sports and pleasures, are self-evidently wise precautions.

Conclusion

It has been our endeavor to set before the vocal student the fundamental principles of the technics of the *Bel Canto* in a concise form. In closing, a few general observations are to be made. What is the best age to begin study, and how long ought one to take lessons? Neither question can be answered off-hand, as all sorts of subordinate points also require consideration. A young man should begin when his voice is fully developed, after reaching, say, the age of twenty. As for the female voice, there is no reason (except a possible consideration of physical development) why training should not begin as early as possible, let us say in the seventeenth year. It was formerly the custom to study at least four or five years, even in Italy, the land of songful speech; nowadays, the shortest course is usually thought the best, with consequences everywhere in evidence. Perfect development alone should be the ideal. Then away with all high-flown schemes and foolish illusions, bringing bitter disappointment in their train! A good education—thorough mental training—will aid the artist everywhere in his future career, and prove of the greatest advantage. And all anemics, and persons with weak lungs or heart, should practise vocal gymnastics, at least, for from four to six months under the supervision of an instructor; for the exercises in deep breathing required by art-vocalism not only expand the chest and strengthen the pectoral muscles and lung-tissue, but also promote in particular the general circulation of the blood, the heart-action, and the change of matter. (These last remarks are addressed especially to young women of weakly physique.) While speaking of vocal delivery, we emphasized the value of a knowledge of the general theory of music, including the intervals. Ability to play the piano is not absolutely essential, but is a great advantage to the singer, who will then not always be dependent upon the accompanist. But it would overtax his physical strength to add any considerable piano-practice to his strenuous vocal studies; either one study or the other! The human voice is the most precious of musical instruments, and more delicate than any other. Only a singer who can sing well is able to endow it with sustained force and expressiveness. It is a matter of but a short series of successive tones—yet what a difference in effect between the finished artist and a bungler! The singer who is once in possession of a perfectly trained voice, will preserve this inestimable treasure till an advanced age. How rich a reward for a few years of sensible and diligent study, reinforced by an orderly mode of life! So away with all artificialities and reckless theorizing; let us return to the simple, natural method!